New Netherland Settlers: The Boelen Family

Ancestry of the Boelen Family & their Connection to the Ten Eyck, Clock, Coert, Roos, and Hellaken Families

By Lorine McGinnis Schulze

ISBN: 978-1-987938-29-6

Publisher Olive Tree Genealogy

Cover Image: Seal of New Netherland

The Seal of New Netherland created in 1623 displays a beaver with the legend SIGILLVM NOVI BELGII (The Seal of New Netherland). The crown at the summit represents the colony's royal Dutch source, while the rampant beaver on the empty field indicates the colony's activity of fur trading. The surrounding necklace of shells is wampum, symbol of the colony's wealth.

DEDICATION

This book is dedicated to my father Cecil Norman McGinnis.

Without the past we cannot build a future.

TABLE OF CONTENTS

BOELE ROELOFFSEN AND HIS WIFE BAYKEN ARENTS IN AMSTERDAM

The descendants of Boele Roeloffsen and his wife Bayken Arents were thoroughly discussed by Howard S. F. Randolph in his article *"Jacob Boelen, Goldsmith, and His Family Circle"* [1] but no attempt was made to document their origins in the Netherlands.

Boele, his wife, and three children arrived from the Netherlands on 12 February 1659 on board *The Otter*.[2] Accompanying them was Bayken's sister, Tryntie Arents, who, within a few months of arrival, was betrothed to Gerrit Jansen Roos. [3]

The entry for their passage read:

"Boele Roeloffsz Jongerman, wife and three children, 2 and 3 years old, the other a nursing child, besides his wife's sister and a boy 14 years old." [4]

Mr. Randolph speculated that the use of Jongerman may have indicated an established surname for Boele. While Jongerman can be translated literally as *"younger man"* and Boele used his patronymic of Roeloffsen in all other records found to date, Jongerman as his surname is a possibility we cannot discount.

The marriage records of the Dutch Reformed Church in New Amsterdam indicate that two of Boele's children, Aefje and Jacob, were born in Amsterdam. [5] Mr. Randolph speculated that Aefjie Boelen was likely the 3 year old in the 1659 passage, and Jacob Boelen was likely the 2 year old. The third (nursing) child who accompanied Boele and Bayken in 1659 has not been found in the records of New Amsterdam, nor until now has this child's name or gender been identified.

In his article, Mr. Randolph speculated that Boele was also the individual whose name appears on the passenger list of *De Sint Pieter* (The St. Peter) arriving from the Netherlands on 16 Oct. 1663, as *"Boele Roeloffsz, farmer, from Friesland"* [6] . Since we know from his marriage intentions that Boele was from Uffelte in the province of Drenthe [7] and not from Friesland, and was a tailor, not a farmer, it is unlikely that this is the same man.

Research undertaken on my behalf at the Gemeentearchief Amsterdam[8] (The Municipal Archive of Amsterdam) by Monique Peters, a Dutch researcher, revealed new information regarding Boele and his family. Boele and Bayken's notice of intent to marry occured 23 April 1654. [9]

(Ze zijn ondertrouwd in de Gereformeerde Kerk)
Den 23 April 1654

Compareerden als vooren Boele Roelofse van uffelt, kleermakergesel out 29 jaer ouders doot wonende op de Kolk geassisteerd met Hendrick Hendrickse ende Baycke Arents van A(msterdam) out 32 jaer wonende op 't Rockin, ouders doot geassisteerd met Luijtje Jans.
(getekend)
boele roelefs   Baijken arens

Translation
(Notice of Marriage in the Protestant Church)
23rd of April 1654

Appeared as before, Boele Roelofse from Uffelt, journeyman tailor, [10] 29 years old, his parents (are) dead, living on the Kolk, assisted by Hendrick Hendrickse and Baycke Arents from Amsterdam, 32 years old, living on the Rokin, her parents (are) dead, assisted by Luitje Jans.
(signed)
boele roelefs   Baijken arens

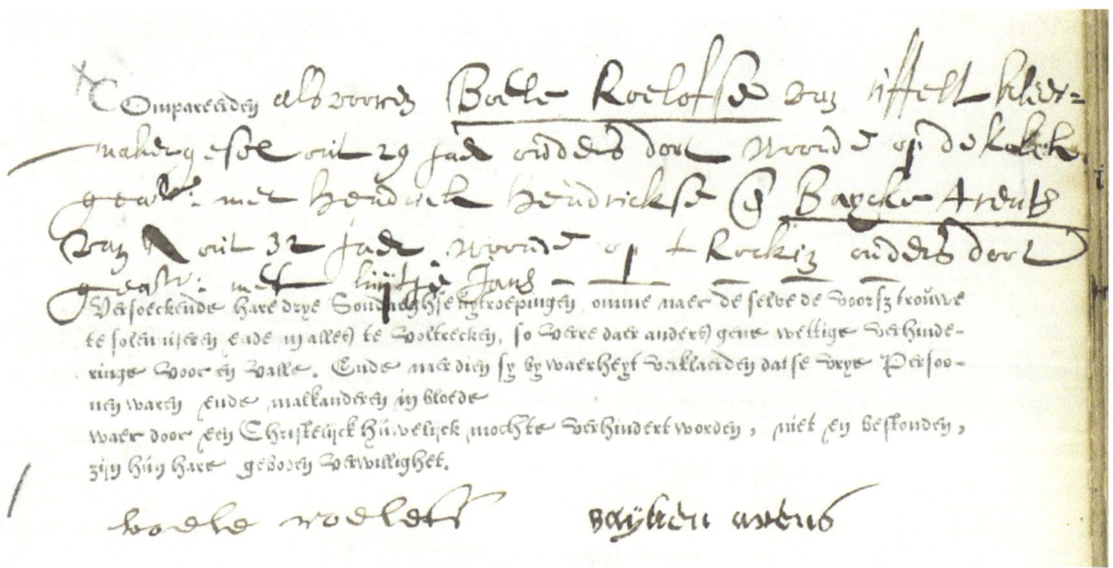

23-04-1654 - Roelofse, Boele - Arents, Baijcke - [11]

Almost three weeks later, on 10 May 1654, Boele Roelofse and Baijke Arents were married in the Nieuwe Kerk [12]

Baptismal records were found in the Nieuwe Kerk for the three children who accompanied Boele Roeloffsen and Bayken Arentse on their 1659 voyage. The children were:

22 March 1655
Child: ***Aefje***

Father Boele Roelofs
Mother Baeijcke Arents.
Sponsor Marije [illegible] [13]

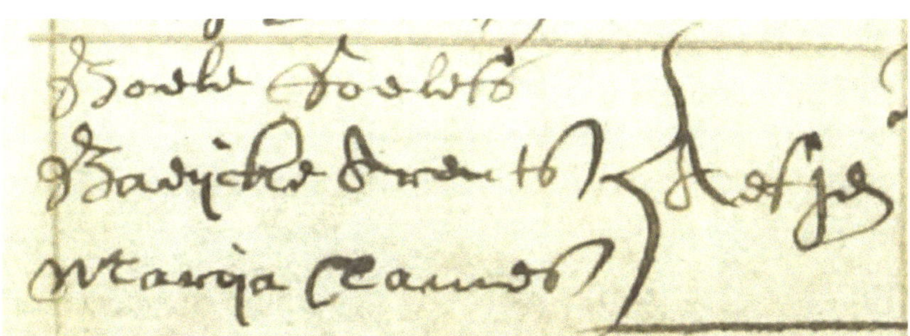

Aefje - 22-03-1655 - Nieuwe Kerk - Hervormd - Roelefs, Boele - Arents, Baeijcke - [14]

25 April 1657
Child: ***Jacob***
Father. Boele Roelofsz
Mother Baijcke Arents
Sponsor Trijnte Arents [probably Bayken's sister who accompanied them on the 1659 voyage][15]

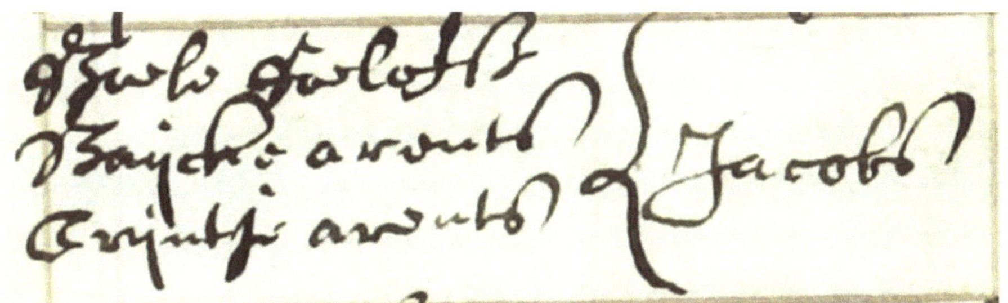

Jacob - 25-04-1657 - Nieuwe Kerk - Hervormd - Roelofsz, Boele - Arents, Baijcke - [16]

11 December 1658
Child: ***Abram***
Father Boele Roelofsz
Mother Baijke Arents
Sponsor Trijnte Arents [probably Bayken's sister] [17]

Abram - 11-12-1658 - Nieuwe Kerk - Hervormd - Roelofsz, Boele - Arents, Baijke [18]

BAYKEN ARENTS & HER ANCESTRY

When Baycke Arents married Boele Roeloffsen in May 1654 she gave her age as 32 years. With the knowledge that Bayken was born circa 1622 in Amsterdam, it was possible to search the records for her birth. Only two baptismal records were found for a Baijken Arents. One was the baptism of Bijcken on 20 October 1624 to Arent Arentsz in the Lutheran Church (no mother named) [19] and the second a baptism of Baijke on 21 March 1621 to Arent Pietersz and Aechjen Heinrixdr. in the Oude Kerk.

The Baijke baptised in March 1621 was 33 in 1654, while the Bijcken baptised in October 1624 was three years younger. The baptism of Baijke in 1621 took place in the Protestant Oude Kerk, Bayken and Boele married in the Protestant Nieuwe Kerk, and their three children born in Amsterdam were baptised in the Protestant Nieuwe Kerk. For these reasons I suggest that the Baijke Arents baptised in March 1621 was most likely the Baycke Arents who married Boele Roeloffsen.

The baptism of Baijke in the Oude Kerk on 21 March 1621 is recorded as:

Child: Baijke
Father: Arent Pietersz
Mother: Aechjen Heinrixdr.
Sponsor: Marijtjen [illegible] [20]

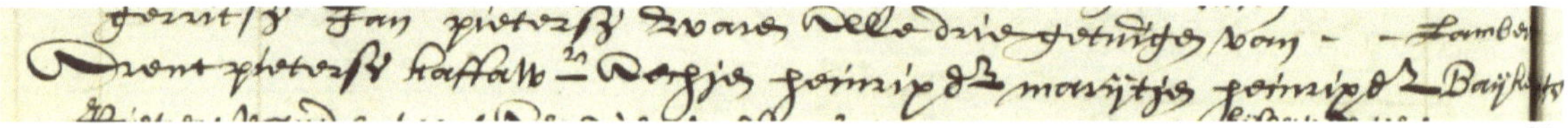

, Baijke - 21-03-1621 - Oude Kerk - Hervormd - Pietersz, Arent - Heinrix, Aechjen - [21]

Arent Pietersz's profession is given as "*Kaffawerker*" which is a worker who made multi-coloured cotton cloth, possibly for export to the Dutch East Indies. [22]

Tryntie Arent's, Bayken's sister, is most likely the Trijntje baptised in the Lutheran Church 18 January 1629 to Arent Pietersz (no mother's name mentioned):

Child: Trijntgen
Father: Arent Pietersz
Sponsor: Grietgen Pieters [23]

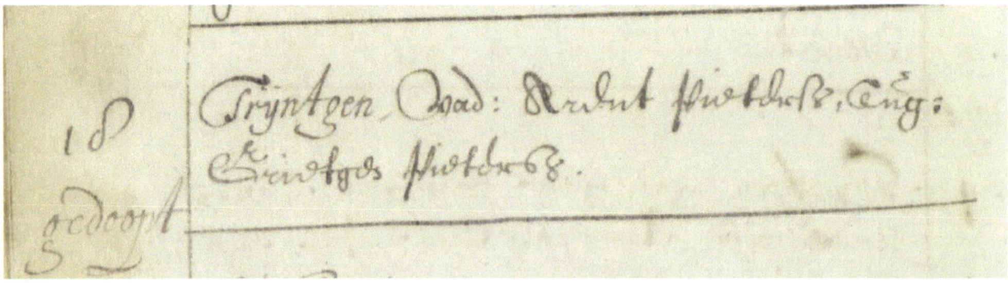

Trijntgen - 18-01-1629 - Lutherse Kerk - Evangelisch-Luthers - Pietersz, Arent - [24]

Continued research found more information on Bayken and her ancestry.

Bayken's father Arent Pietersz was sometimes recorded with a second name, Arent Roukesz. Some Dutch individuals had an established surname and would use that in place of their patronymic. A search of the Amsterdam records found the marriage of Bayken's parents Arent Pieterse Roukens and Aechjen Heinrixdr. in 1610

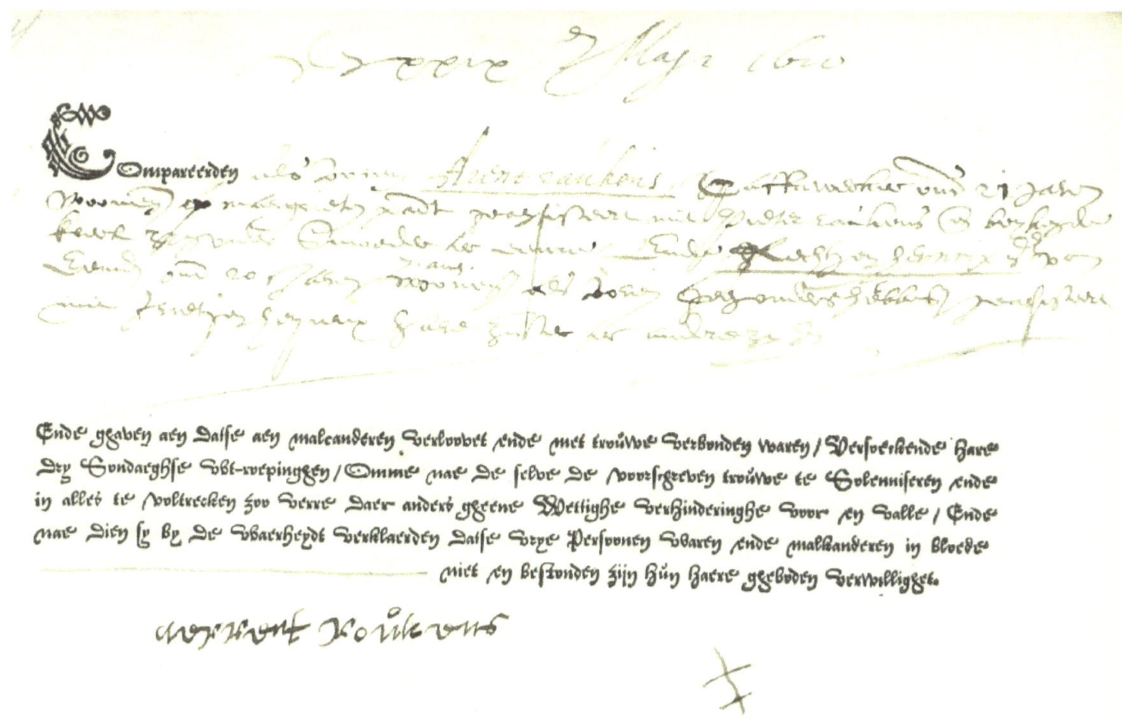

Ende gaven an dasse an malcanderen verloobt ende met trouwe verbonden waren / Versoeckende haer drij Sondaeghse Uyt-roepinghen / Omme nae de selve de voorschreven trouwe te Solenniseren ende in alles te voltrecken zoo verre daer anders gheene Wettighe verhinderinghe voor en valle / Ende nae dien sy by de waerheydt verklaerden dat sy vrye Persoonen waren ende malkanderen in bloede niet en bestonden zijn hun haere gheboden verwilligt.

29-05-1610 - Roukens, Arent - Heijnrix, Aachtje - [25]

Marriage Record, 1610, May 29. [26] Arent Roukens 21 years old (born ca 1589) and Aachtie Heynrix, 20 years old (born ca 1590) Pieter Roukens named as father of Arent.

Baptismal records in Amsterdam revealed three more children for Arent and Aechjie, giving Bayken two brothers and a sister.

Barber - 12-06-1611 - Oude Kerk - Hervormd - Rokesz, Arent - Heinrix, Aechjen - DTB 4, p.352 – 000000033678

Frans - 15-07-1612 - Nieuwe Kerk - Hervormd - Roukes, Arent - Henrix, Aechje - DTB 39, p.290 – 000000040981

Pieter - 01-02-1615 - Oude Kerk - Hervormd - Roukesz, Arent - Heinrix, Aecht - DTB 5, p.131 - A28217000069

Pieter married Grietje Willems in 1636. As the widower of Grietje Willems he married Elsje Claes Witt in 1641

06-09-1636 - Arentss, Pieter - Willems, Grietje - DTB 445, p.121 - Huwelijksintekeningen van de KERK. - OTR00032000067

15-06-1641 - Rokusz, Pieter Arent - Willems, Grietje - Witt, Elsje Claes - DTB 456, p.45 - Huwelijksintekeningen van de KERK. - OTR00041000025

PIETER FRANSSEN ROUCKENS

Arent Rouken's father Pieter Fransen Rouken married Barber Claes before 1589. Two children were found for this couple in the Amsterdam church records.

Aerent - 21-05-1589 - Oude Kerk - Hervormd - Franssen, Pieter - Croech, Barber - DTB 2, p.15 - Zijdewerker – 000000033205

Pouwels - 04-02-1592 - Nieuwe Kerk - Hervormd - Fransen, Pieter - Claes, Berber - DTB 38, p.229 - 000000040462

Some time between February 1592 and August 1593 Pieter may have married Maijke Jansen. The following children were found in the Amsterdam records.

Tanneken - 22-08-1593 - Nieuwe Kerk - Hervormd - Fransen, Pieter - Fransen, Maeicke - DTB 38, p.306 - 000000040501

Pieter - 24-06-1595 - Nieuwe Kerk - Hervormd - Fransen, Pieter - Jans, Maeicke - DTB 38, p.424 - ber. va. Droogscheerder – 000000040560

Barbertge - 13-07-1603 - Nieuwe Kerk - Hervormd - Franse, Pieter - Jans, Maijke - DTB 39, p.13 - 000000040842

PATRONYMICS

The most common Dutch naming custom was that of patronymics, or identification of an individual based on his/her father's name. For example, Jan Albertszen is named after his father, Albert. Albertszen means son of a man named Albert. The patronymic was formed by adding -se, -sen, -szen and –sz.

The patronymic ending for women was formed by adding –s, or -sdr. Women were sometimes recorded under their husband's name, thus forming a husband-o-nymic of sorts. For example, Maria Goosens (Maria, daughter of a man named Goosen) was sometimes recorded as Maria Jans (Jans being the feminine version of her husband Steven Janszen's patronymic).

An individual could also be known by his place of origin. For example, Cornelis Antoniszen was known in some records as 'van Breuckelen', meaning 'from Breuckelen' (Breuckelen being a town in the Netherlands). The place-origin name could be a nationality, as in the case of Albert Andriessen from Norway, originator of the Bradt and Vanderzee families. He is entered in many records as Albert Andriessen de Noorman, meaning Albert, son of Andries, the Norseman (Norwegian).

An individual might be known by a personal characteristic, for e.g. Vrooman means a wise man; Krom means bent or crippled; De Witt means the white one. Maria Goosens was called Lange Mary (tall Mary) and is found as such in several records of the day. A fascinating example is that of Pieter Adrianszen (Peter, son of Adrian) who was given the nickname of Soo Gemackelyck (so easy-going) but was also known as Pieter Van Waggelen/Van Woggelum from his place of origin. His children adopted the surnames Mackelyck and Woglom.

Sometimes an occupation became the surname. For example Smit meant a (black)Smith; Schenck was a cupbearer, Metsalaer was a mason, Cuyper was a barrelmaker.

An individual might be known by many different 'surnames' - and entered in official records under these different names, making the search difficult unless you're aware of the names in use. For e.g. Cornelis Antoniszen mentioned above was known, and written of, under the following names:

Cornelis Antoniszen
Cornelis Teuniszen (Teunis being the diminuitive of Antony)
Cornelis Antoniszen/Teuniszen van Breuckelen
Cornelis Antoniszen/Teuniszen Van Slicht (this is how he signed his name and was likely a hereditary family name based on an old place of origin)
Broer Cornelis (name given him by Mohawks and meaning "Brother Cornelis" in Dutch))

There were also differences over the generations. Albert's sons and daughters took the surname Bradt except for his son Storm, born on the Atlantic Ocean during the family's sailing to the New World. Storm adopted the surname Vanderzee (from the sea) and this is the name his descendants carry.

The Dutch were much slower in adopting surnames as we know them than the English. Patronymics ended, theoretically, some time around 1687 but not everyone followed the new guidelines.

You must also be aware of the diminutives of regular first names, because the patronymic might be formed from the normal name or its diminuitive. For e.g.:

Antonis	Theunis/Teunis
Matthys	Thys/Tice
Harmanus	Harman, Manus
Jacobus	Cobus
Nicolas	Claes
Denys	Nys
Bartolomeus	Bartol, Meese/Meus
Cornelis	Krelis, Kees

In the case of Steven Janse, he is found in official records of the day as:

Steven Janszen
Steven Janszen, Timmerman (carpenter)
Steven Janszen Coninck (King)

Steven's male children, whose patronymic was Stevensen, had their patronymics frozen as a surname (sometimes called a petrified patronymic), and descendants carry this name.

TRANSLATION OF DUTCH PHRASES IN CHURCH RECORDS

Wonende in [location]	Living in [location]
Overt 't Versche Water	Across the fresh water
Beyde wonende alhier	Both of them living here (at this town)
Beyde op (name) bouwerye	Both on (name) farm
Als voren	As before (as previously stated)
Beyde wonende tot [name of place]	Both living at [name of place]
D'Eerste wonende alhier, entwede tot [name of place]	The first one living here (at this town) and the second one at [name of place)
Met Attestatie getrouwt op [name of place]	Married with certificate at [name of place]
Vertoog Verleent, om te trouwen tot [name of place]	a note was given(granted) in order to marry at [name of place]
Met vertoog	With permission
Gertrouwt	married
Ingeschreven	Registered, name entered on a list
Gestorven	deceased
Vertrocken	left, moved out
Vertrocken na	vertrokken na=left after (time)
Verongeluckt	died because of an accident
Vertrocken met attest Na [name of place]	left with documents of proof of belonging to a Church to [name of place]
en	and
syn	his
s. huys vrow	his wife
z.h.v. (zijne huis vrouw)	his wife
s.h.VR (zijne huis vrouw)	his wife
s.h.v. (sijne huis vrouw)	his wife
huis v. van (huisvrouw van)	wife of
huys v. van (huis vrouw van)	wife of
j.d. (jonge dochter)	unmarried woman
j.m. (jonge man)	unmarried man

ORIGINS OF NEW NETHERLAND

On September 19, 1609, the East India Company ship *Halve Maen (Half Moon)*, commanded by Henry Hudson, an Englishman working for Dutch businessmen who were seeking a passage to the Orient, reached the present-day Albany area. He had started up the Hudson River just 8 days earlier, on September 11. As the *Half Moon* lay at anchor, Hudson could see an island lying between two rivers to his north. To the west was a vast, unexplored wooded land.

In 1613, four years after Henry Hudson explored the river that now bears his name, a Dutch ship called the *Tiger* left Holland en route for the same waters. Adriaen Block, the captain, was an enterprising Dutchman who had made two earlier visits to these waters. The market for furs in Europe was growing, and Block's earlier visits had convinced him that he could fill his ship with furs which he could sell in the Netherlands as coats and hats.

Two months after he left the Netherlands, Block passed through the narrows that guard the entrance to what is now New York Harbour. Within a few weeks he was anchored at the southern tip of modern-day Manhattan Island, his ship filled with beaver and otter pelts. Unfortunately for Block and his men, the *Tiger* caught fire and burned. Block and his crew were stranded thousands of miles from home. Over the long difficult winter, Block and his men built a new ship, a 44 foot sailing vessel they named the *Restless.*

Cutting down trees and using whatever tools they could salvage from the *Tiger*, the men completed the ship by the spring of 1614 and prepared to sail home. It was on this return voyage that Block and his men discovered Long Island Sound. Block sailed into a freshwater river he named Fresh River (present day Connecticut River) and then dropped anchor at a place he called Hoeck van de Visschers or Point of the Fishers (present day Montauk Point). Having sailed completely around the long island, he claimed it for the Netherlands.

On reaching the Netherlands, Block appeared before government officials. After hearing his story they named the area he had surveyed (from Chesapeake Bay to Cape Cod) *Nieuw Nederlandt (*New Netherland*).* The name *Nieuw Nederlandt* appeared for the first time on October 11, 1614 in a resolution of the States General of the United Provinces. A charter concerning trading licenses between New France and Virginia was issued to merchants to begin trading, and a settlement was planned for the island where Block had built the *Restless.*

The goal of this newly formed New Netherland Company was to sponsor voyages to the area between 40 and 45 degrees north latitude -- the middle of present-day New Jersey to the coast of Maine. This huge region now had a formal, European name.

It wasn't long before the Dutch started construction on a log fort on an island at the northernmost part of the Hudson River that was navigable for their ships. This was near present-day Albany. At about the same time, merchants in the Netherlands formed a second business entity for the purposes of exploiting their new fur-rich land. This was the Charter of the Dutch West India Company (commonly referred to as the WIC) which was chartered by the States General on 3 June 1621.

The West India Company was designed to stand strong against Spain's interests in the New World. It was empowered to create colonies, settle people, attack Spanish vessels, conduct trade and make treaties with the Indians. The Province of New Netherland fell under the broad monopoly of this company. The capital of New Netherland was to be established on Manhattan Island and called New Amsterdam.

After the charter of the West India Company in 1621, Fort Orange was built. It was built as a redoubt, surrounded by a moat 18 feet wide, mounted with 2 cannons and 11 pederos, and garrisoned by 10 to 12 men. Around this was clustered a tiny hamlet occupied by the factors and servants of the WIC, who claimed all rights to the entire Indian trade. Although the charter, stated in part that they were to "*....advance the peopling of those fruitful and unsettled parts*", colonization was not encouraged.

The first interest of the Dutch in the Netherlands was the fur trade. Thus the New World represented a business opportunity. By 1624 Dutch traders were establishing the fort near Albany. English colonists were in Virginia and Plymouth, and England was claiming the northeastern Atlantic Coast. Both the English and the Dutch laid claim to Long Island, where the Dutch took hold of the western end, and later, the English settled on the eastern end.

To bolster their own land claims, the Dutch began to establish more settlements. They sent groups of Walloons (French-speaking refugees from Belgium) to New Netherland. The first group of Walloons arrived on *Niew Nederlandt* in 1624 when approximately 30 families arrived. By 1626, these groups had a stronghold on Manhattan Island.

Peter Minuit arrived in New Netherland aboard the *See Meeuw* on May 4, 1626 to become Director of the Colony. He purchased Manhattan from the local Indians for 60 guilders' worth of trade goods. He ordered that the settlement should be located on the southern portion of Manhattan Island.

The Schaghen letter is the earliest reference to this this purchase. Peter Schaghen, the author, was the representative of the States General in the Assembly of the Nineteen of the West India Company. In the late summer of 1626 he reported the arrival of the ship *Wapen van Amsterdam* (Arms of Amsterdam) from New Netherland. In his report to the directors of the West India Company he announced the purchase of Manhattan Island for the value of 60 guilders. The original of this document is held by the Rijksarchief in The Hague. A copy of the document along with the English translation follows:

Rcvd. 7 November 1626

High and Mighty Lords,

Yesterday the ship the Arms of Amsterdam arrived here. It sailed from New Netherland out of the River Mauritius on the 23d of September. They report that our people are in good spirit and live in peace. The women also have borne some children there. They have purchased the Island Manhattes from the Indians for the value of 60 guilders. It is 11,000 morgens in size [about 22,000 acres]. They had all their grain sowed by the middle of May, and reaped by the middle of August They sent samples of these summer grains: wheat, rye, barley, oats, buckwheat, canary seed, beans and flax. The cargo of the aforesaid ship is:

7246 Beaver skins

178½ Otter skins

675 Otter skins

48 Mink skins

36 Lynx skins

33 Minks

34 Weasel skins

Many oak timbers and nut wood. Herewith, High and Mighty Lords, be commended to the mercy of the Almighty,

Your High and Mightinesses' obedient, P.Schaghen

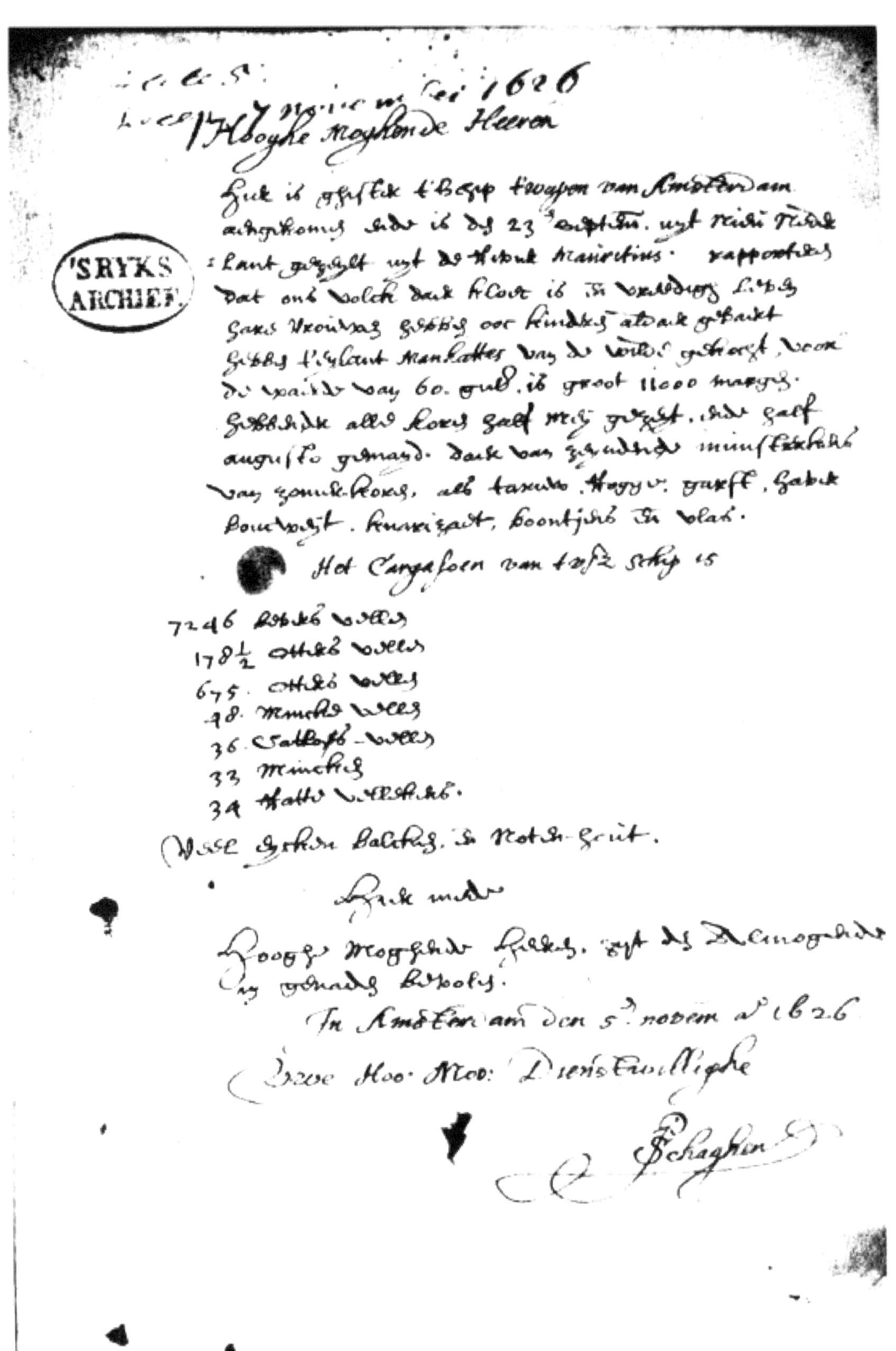
Recepi 7 novem 1626

Hooghe Moghende Heeren

Hier is gisteren t'schip t'wapen van Amsterdam aengecomen ende is den 23 septbr. uyt Nieu Nederlant gezeylt uyt de Rivier Mauritius. rapporteren dat ons volck daer kloec is, en vredich leven. haere vrouwen hebben oock kinderen aldaer gebaert hebben t'eylant Manhattes van de wilde gekocht, voor de waerde van 60. guld. is groot 11000 morgen. hebben alle koren half mey gezaeyt. ende half augusto gemaeyd. daer van sijn monsterkens van somer koren, als tarwe, rogge, garst, haver, boeckweyt, knariezaet, boontjes en vlas.

Het Cargasoen van tselve schip is

7246 bevers vellen
178½ otters vellen
675 otters vellen
48 mincke vellen
36 catlossen vellen
33 mincken
34 ratte vellekens.

Veele eycken balcken en noten hout.

Hiermede

Hooge Moghende Heeren, sijt den Almogende in genade bevolen.

In Amsterdam den 5en novem ao 1626

Uwe Hoo: Moo: Dienstwillighe

P. Schaghen

Courtesy of New Netherland Project, New York State Library

Soon a tiny community was built on the southern tip of Manhattan Island and called New Amsterdam by the Dutch. It was walled off to the north by a thick forest laced with Indian trails. Trees were cut down and small houses were erected. Dirt cart paths became streets. Windmills for making flour were built at the tops of creeks; sailing vessels lined new docksides. To the east, across what is today's East River, lay Long Island.

There was too much to be gained financially by not allowing further colonization. Eventually the Directors in Amsterdam were forced to find a remedy. On the 7th of June 1629, under the title of *Freedoms and Exemptions*, Patroons, those individuals authorized to establish plantations in Dutch New Netherland, were given freedom to bring colonists to New Netherland. Anyone who shipped 50 colonists to the New World at his own expense could buy land along the Hudson River. This man, called a Patroon, had complete jurisdiction and full trade privileges (excluding furs) in perpetuity for himself and his heirs. Thus a type of feudal system was begun in the New World.

The Directors in Holland rushed to avail themselves of the privileges; for the Charter offered them profit and gratification. WIC officials mainly wanted to make a fast profit and return home. They had the monopoly on the fur trade; so the Patroons had a slower rate of return from their initial investment, as well as losses from shipwrecks and Indian raids. By 1635 four of the five original Patroonships had failed, with the only remaining (and successful) one being Rensselaerswyck, run by Kiliaen van Rensselaer from the Netherlands.

The failure of the West India Company and the Patroons to fulfill the requirements of their charter with respect to colonization and encouragement of agriculture was so great that in 1638 the States-General was called on. The Directors were forced to proclaim free trade (including the all-important fur trade) and free lands to private persons under certain restrictions. This had the happy effect of stimulating immigration to New Netherland from the Netherlands. Willem Kieft arrived on board *De Haring* on March 28, 1638 to assume the directorship of New Netherland. One year later an enumeration of buildings erected for the West India Company on the Island of Manhattan, at Pavonia, The Bay, and Forts Orange, Nassau and Hope was completed.

Kieft's tenure from 1638 to 1647 was ruinous. As an administrator he was incompetent, and he did not accept any opposition.

By 1643 Kieft, in his lust for more land, had managed single-handedly to start a large-scale war, named the Kieft War. In 1643 war broke out across Manhattan and western Long Island that resulted in more than 1,000 Indian deaths, including a massacre in what is today Massapequa. Although several of Kieft's Officers objected to the plan to attack the starving and destitute refugees who had fled from their Mohawk enemies, Kieft insisted and on 23 February 1643 his men attacked with the resulting massacre leaving over 100 Indians dead. The results on the inhabitants of

New Netherland was devastating as the remaining Indians quickly retaliated. Willem Kieft, recalled in disgrace to the Netherlands, was lost at sea on board the ill-fated *Princess* on his return trip in 1647. The Princess, carrying approximately 100 passengers, including Kieft, his next in command Cornelis Melyn, one of Kieft's most vocal opponents Domine Everardus Bogardus, and others, floundered off the coast of Wales and sank. Fewer than 20 men were saved; the rest, including Kieft and Bogardus, perished.

Of the earliest settlers, more than half were French speaking Walloons from what is now Belgium. Father Joque, a Jesuit missionary from New France (present day Quebec province) who was visiting the village in 1644 noted only ten thatched cottages. He also reported that there were four hundred people in New Amsterdam and 18 different languages.

Father Jogue wrote to his supervisors in France:

New Netherlands in 1644

By Rev. Isaac Jogues, S.J.

New Holland which the Dutch call in Latin Novum Belgium, in their own language Nieuw Nederland, that is to say, New Low Countries, is situated between Virginia and New England. The mouth of the river called by some Nassau river or the great North river (to distinguish it from another which they call the South river) and which in some maps that I have recently seen is also called, I think, River Maurice, is at 40°30'. Its channel is deep, for the largest ships that ascend to Manhattes Island, which is seven leagues in circuit, and on which there is a fort to serve as the commencement of a town to be built there and to be called New Amsterdam.

This fort which is at the point of the island about five or six leagues from the mouth, is called Fort Amsterdam; it has four regular bastions mounted with several pieces or artillery. All these bastions and the curtains were in 1643 but ramparts of earth, most of which had crumbled away, so that the fort could be entered on all sides. There were no ditches. There were sixty soldiers to garrison the said fort and anotherwhich they had built still further up against the incursions of the savages their enemies. They were beginning to face the gates and bastions with stone. Within this fort stood a pretty large church built of stone; the house of the Governor, whom they called Director General, quite neatly built of brick, the storehouses and barracks.

On this island of Manhate and in its environs there may well be four or five hundred men of different sects and nations; the Director General told me that there were persons there of eighteen different languages; they are scattered here and there on the river, above and below as the beauty and convenience of the spot invited each to settle, some mechanics however who ply their trades are ranged under the fort; all the others were exposed to the incursions of the natives, who in the year 1643, while I was there actually killed some two score Hollanders and burnt many houses and barns full of wheat.

The river, which is very straight and runs due north and south, is at least a league broad before the fort. Ships lie at anchor in a bay which forms the other side of the island and can be defended from the fort.

Shortly before I arrived there three large vessels of 300 tons each had come to load wheat; two had found cargoes, the third could not be loaded because the savages had burnt a part of their grain. These ships came from the West Indies where the West India Company usually keeps up seventeen ships of war.

No religion is publicly exercised but the Calvinist, and orders are to admit none but Calvinists, but this is not observed, for there are, besides Calvinists, in the Colony Catholics, English Puritans, Lutherans, Anabaptists, here called Muistes &c.

When any one comes to settle in the country, they lend him horses, cows &c, they give him provisions, all which he repays as soon as he is at ease, and as to the land he pays in to the West India Company after ten years the tenth of the produce which he reaps.

This country is bounded on the New England side by a river they call the Fresche river, which serves as a boundary between them and the English. The English however come very near to them, preferring to hold lands under the Dutch who ask nothing from them rather than to be dependant on English Lords who exact rents and would fain be absolute. On the other side southward towards Virginia, its limits are the river which they call the South river on which there is also a Dutch settlement, but the Swedes have at its mouth another extremely well provided with men and cannon. It is believed that these Swedes are maintained by some merchants of Amsterdam, who are not satisfied that the West India Company should alone enjoy all the commerce of these parts. It is near this river that a gold mine is reported to have been found.

See in the work of the Sieur de Laet of Antwerp the table and article on New Belgium as he sometimes calls it or the map; Nova Anglia, Novu Belgium et Virginia.

It is about fifty years since the Hollanders came to these parts. The fort was begun in the year 1615: they began to settle about twenty years ago and there is already some little commerce with Virginia and New England.

The first comers found lands fit for use, formerly cleared by the savages who previously had fields here. Those who came later have cleared in the woods, which are mostly of oak. The soil is good. Deer hunting is abundant in the fall. There are some houses built of stone; they make lime of oyster shells, great heaps of which are found here made formerly by the savages, who subsisted in part by this fishery.

The climate is very mild. Lying at 40 2/3 degrees; there are many European fruits, as apples, pears, cherries. I reached there in October, and found even then a considerable quantity of peaches.

Ascending the river to the 43d degree you find the second Dutch settlement, which the flux and reflux reaches but does not pass. Ships of a hundred and a hundred and twenty tons can ascend to it. There are two things in this settlement, which is called Renselaerswick, as if to say the colony of Renselaer, who is a rich Amsterdam merchant: 1st a wretched little fort called Ft Orange, built of logs with four or five pieces of cannon of Breteuil and as many swivels. This has been reserved and is maintained by the West Indis Company. This fort was formerly on an island in the river, it is now on the main land towards the Hiroquois, a little above the said island. 2ndly, a colonie sent here by this Renselaer, who is the Patroon. This colonie is composed of about a hundred persons, who resident in some 25 or 30 houses, built along the river, as each one found it most convenient. In the principal house resides the Patroon's agent, the minister has his apart, in which service is performed. There is also a kind of bailiff here whom they call Seneschal, who administers justice. All their houses are merely of boards and thatched. As yet there is no mason work, except in the chimneys. The forests furnishing many large pines, they make boards by means of their mills which they have for the purpose.

They found some pieces of ground all ready, which the savages had formerly prepared and in which they sow wheat and oats for beer and for their horses, of which they have a great stock. There is little land fit for tillage, being crowded by hills which are bad soil. This obliges them to be separated the one from the other, and they occupy already two or three leagues of country.

Trade is free to all, this gives the Indians all things cheap, each of the Hollanders outbidding his neighbor and being satisfied provided he can gain some little profit.

This settlement is not more than twenty leagues from the Agniehronons, who can be reached either by land or by water, as the river on which the Iroquois lie falls into that which passes by the Dutch; but there are many shallow rapids and a fall of a short half league where the canoe has to be carried.

There are many nations between the two Dutch settlements, which are about thirty German leagues apart, that is about 50 or 60 French leagues. The Loups, whom the Iroquois call Agotzogenens, are the nearest to Renselaerwick and Ft Orange. War breaking out some years ago between the Iroquois and the Loups, the Dutch joined the latter against the former, but four having been taken and burnt they made peace. Some nations near the sea having murdered some Hollanders of the most distant settlement, the Hollanders killed 150 Indians, men, women and children; the latter having killed at divers intervals 40 Dutchmen, burnt several houses and committed ravages, estimated at the time that I was there at 200,000 liv. (two hundred thousand livres) troops were raised in New England, and in the beginning of winter the grass being low and some snow on the ground they pursued them with six hundred men, keeping two hundred always on the move and constantly relieving each other, so that the Indians, pent up in a large island and finding it impossible to escape, on account of the women and children, were cut to pieces to the number of sixteen hundred, women and children included. This obliged the rest of the Indians to make peace, which still continues. This occurred in 1643 and 1644.

Three Rivers in New France,
August 3d, 1646.

On May 11, 1647 Petrus Stuyvesant arrived at Manhattan with the West India Company ships *Groote Gerrit* and *Princess Amalia* to assume his position as Director General of New Netherland. This position included the colonies at Curaçao, Bonaire and Aruba. At the start of Stuyvesant's administration, the population of New Netherland was an estimated 1,000 to 8,000. There is no exact count of the population at that time and only rough estimates can be made. By 1664 it was 10,000.

When he first arrived, Stuyvesant realized that English settlers were spilling into Dutch areas, so in 1650 he negotiated a treaty in Hartford. This treaty drew a line that began near present-day Greenwich, Connecticut, and crossed Long Island, beginning just west of what is now Oyster Bay. West of this line was Dutch, east of it was English.

In the early 1650s, the Dutch and English began fighting in Europe over trade and naval supremacy. This tension spilled over to the New World, where by the mid-1660s the English were trying to oust the Dutch from New Netherland. Locally, there was a desire for more territory and the English were encroaching the Dutch borders.

In 1656 the WIC decided that "all mechanics and farmers who can prove their ability to earn a living here [New Netherland] shall receive free passage for themselves, their wives, and children" Colonists were granted as much land as they could cultivate, but without the privileges Patroons had formerly held. The result was an increase in population from an estimated 2,000 in 1648 to 10,000 in 1660. New Netherland changed during this time from a trading post to a colony.

List of Governors or Director-Generals of New Netherland

1624-1625 Cornelis Jacobsen May
1625-1626 Willem Verhulst
1626-1632 Peter Minuit
1632-1633 Sebastian Jansen Krol
1633-1638 Wouter Van Twiller
1638-1647 Willem Kieft
1647-1664 Peter Stuyvesant

RENSSELAERSWYCK BEGINNINGS

Rensselaerswyck was the name given to the large tract of land granted to the wealthy Dutchman and Patroon, Killiaen Van Rensselaer in 1632. It included all the land that surrounded the present-day city of Albany and was situated on both sides of the Hudson River. The colony of Rensselaerswyck and the West India Company officials had long been involved in disputes over jurisdiction of territory around the Fort. When the patroon of Rensselaerswyck claimed all land west of the Hudson River from Beeren Island to Moenemin's Castle (including Fort Orange) had been bought for him. The WIC claimed that the land around the Fort, which had been built six years prior to the patroonship, belonged to the WIC and was not included in the purchase of 1632.

Killiaen Van Rensselaer established a patroonship in the upper Hudson Valley in order to cultivate the land and mine the wilderness for farm and forest products that could be exported to Europe and sold. Before his death in 1643, he hired hundreds of willing pioneers from the Old World and sent them to Rensselaerswyck to be his tenants. These settlers consisted of farmers, artisans, tradesmen, and others who could support the new settlement. Most of Van Rensselaer's tenants settled within a few miles of Fort Orange.

On 10 April 1652, Director General Stuyvesant issued a proclamation. By this proclamation the main settlement of the Colony of Rensselaerswyck was removed from the jurisdiction of the patroon and created as an independent village called Beverwyck. Beverwyck later became Albany. The jurisdiction of the court included Fort Orange, Beverwyck, Schenectady, Kinderhook, Claverack, Coxsackie, Catskill and (until 1661) Esopus (present day Kingston). The Colony of Rensselaerswcyk was not included in this jurisdiction until 1665 when the two courts were ordered to combine.

Rensselaerswyck was the only one of five original Patroonships which was successful.

EARLY SETTLERS & IMMIGRATION

What we call "passenger lists" were in reality account books of credits and debits for voyages. All such "passenger lists" for travel from The Netherlands to New Netherland between 1654 and 1664 are derived from information on the debit side of the West India Company Account Book. Thus the set of "passenger lists" that we have for the years 1654-1664 are from an account book showing who owed money when they arrived. The published lists draw only from the debit side; the credit side has not been published.

Typical fare for passage was 36 florins for each adult; half that for young children; and nothing for nursing infants. Names were not usually recorded except for the person owing the money. Thus we might see an entry such as "Cornelis Jacobszen van Beest, wife and two children ages 11 and 5" with an amount due beside the entry. The ages of children were given in order to determine the fee for passage.

A typical voyage from the Netherlands to New Netherland took between 7 and 8 weeks.

Many of the early shipping records from the West India Company have not survived, and we must use other records to determine who the early settlers were and when they arrived in the colony. One of these is the 1651 Oath of Fidelity to the Patroon in Rensselaerswyck

We can also consult the notarial records held in Amsterdam, Netherlands. Approximately 10% of the total notarial records have been indexed, and they hold a wealth of information. Most early settlers to New Netherland entered into a contract with their employer (the Patroon or the WIC or an established settler with money) before leaving for the New World. Many of these contracts can be found in the Amsterdam Notarial Records and include details such as origin of the settler, contract period (2 to 6 years), wages and other agreed-upon details, and sometimes the name of the ship the settler was to sail on. Even if the name of the ship is not given, the date of the contract is usually a good indicator of the sailing date, as the contracts were entered into shortly before the settler sailed. A search of Jaap Jacobs' list of ships sailing from the Netherlands to the New World (and back) can often provide a strong circumstantial case for an individual's being on board a specific ship.

RELIGION

The established church in the United Netherlands was the Reformed Church. In 1628 the Dutch West India Company sent the Reverend Jonas Michaelius as the first ordained minister to New Netherland. However, even before the arrival of Michaelius, Sebastiaen Jansz Kroll had been sent over in 1624 as a comforter of the sick. Although he began his duties in New Amsterdam, he was soon sent to Fort Orange, arriving there in 1628. The comforters of the sick were required to read prayers every morning and evening, as well as before and after meals, to instruct and comfort the sick, to exhort those who required or requested exhortation, and to read chapters from the Bible and sermons of an ordained minister. The comforters were empowered to baptize and marry, but could not administer Holy Communion. A special form of service was prepared for them to read.

After a few months at Fort Orange, Comforter Krol returned to the Netherlands to obtain a minister for New Netherland. However the settlement was not considered large enough to warrant a minister, and Bastien Krol returned to New Netherland with power to baptize and marry, provided he used the liturgy of the church in his services. When Governor Peter Minuit arrived in 1626 to take charge of the colony, he ordered that the settlement should center about the southern portion of Manhattan Island. Soon after Peter Minuit's order, Comforter Krol left Fort Orange to become the first comforter at New Amsterdam.

In 1632 the *Patroon* Kiliaen van Rensselaer gave instructions that settlers in the Colony of Rensselaerswyck should come together every Sunday and on holidays to read passages and chapters from the Bible. Brant Peele van Niekerck was authorized by van Rensselaer to read from the Bible.

The church founded at Albany in 1640 was the only one north of Esopus with a permanent ministry - other than Schenectady. All babies were baptised and their names entered in the *Doop Boek*, but sadly Albany's records are scanty prior to 1684. Many are lost completely. The population of Fort Orange is not known in this early period, but it was small. The first church built in 1648 was 84x19 feet, and consisted of only nine benches for those attending services. This church was still in use until 1656.

It was not until 1642 that Dominie Johannes Megapolensis was hired to preach in Rensselaerswyck. There was no church building, and it is not known where he held services. In 1649 Dominie Megapolensis was called from Rensselaerwyck (Albany) to assume charge at Manhattan. For the next year, his son-in-law, Dominie Grasmeer, conducted the Albany area services.

The *Patroon's* trading house on the west side of the Hudson River, had been turned into a church in March 1648. The *dominie* was an ordained minister of the Dutch Reformed Church sent by the church leadership in the Netherlands to minister to the Albany congregation. Dominie Gideon Schaets arrived in the Colony in July 1652 and was minister until his death in 1694. Both *dominies* (ministers) and Deacons (lay leaders) staffed the church. The Deacons were prominent Albany businessmen and officials.

In June 1656 the cornerstone of the new Dutch Reformed Church was laid. There are no known surviving registers from the church at Beverwyck/Albany before 1684.

Albany Dutch Reformed Church.
Courtesy New York State Museum

List of Ministers at the Albany Dutch Reformed Church

Johannes Megapolensis, Jr. 1642-52
Gideon Schaets, 1652-1691
Godefridus Dellius, 1683-1699
Johannes Nucella, 1699-1700
Johannes Lydius, 1700-1710
Petrus Van Driessen, 1712-1738
Cornelis Van Schie, 1733-1744
Theodorus Frielinghuysen,1746-59
Eilardus Westerlo, 1760-1790
John Bassett, 1787-1804
John B. Johnson, 1796-1802

MONEY & MONEY SUBSTITUTES IN NEW NETHERLAND

Native Indians did not use currency. Instead they collected oblong shells which they polished and cut into beads. The finished highly polished beads were often attached to clothing. They were used as necklaces, belts and frequently strung in rows. These lengths of shells called *wampum* were often given as gifts. All beads were made up of highly polished cylinders about 1/8 " diameter and ¼" long, drilled length-wise and strung on ropes of hemp or the tendons of animals. While the local area dictated what shells could be used, in general black beads came from the local clam, known as the *quahaug*; while white beads came from winkles or periwinkles.

Indian beads were known by a variety of names among the early colonists - wampum, wampom-peage, wampeage, peage (which referred to beads that were strung), and in some localities such as New Netherland, seawan or seawand. In general the Dutch called it *seawan* (which they used for all shelled money), the English wampum. For the Indians, *wampum* referred strictly to white beads. They called their black beads *suckaubock*. The colonists used what they considered the generic term of *wampum* to refer to both varieties.

In 1609 Hudson's men received strings of beads from local Indians. The first European to use these beads for barter was a Dutch fur trader named Jacob Eelckens. In 1622 Eelckens demanded a ransom for a Pequot *sachem* (chief) on Long Island. The *wampum* Eelckens was given brought him more furs in trade than conventional trade goods. Before long the West India Company, recognizing a good thing, had their agents purchase all the *wampum* they could and take it north to Fort Orange. There they used it to buy furs from the Mahicans. Almost overnight *wampum* was functioning like money.

When Dutch traders encountered *wampum* they adopted it as a money substitute. Although more convenient than commodity money several problems developed with the use of *wampum*. It had no intrinsic value, and anyone could collect some shells and produce their own currency. With no central minting operation the quality of these products was often substandard. Shopkeepers needed to keep a vigilant eye for inferior *wampum* but there was no legislation in place that allowed them to refuse poor quality beads. Further, the amount of *wampum* produced was unregulated, and this eventually caused an oversupply.

In New Netherland *wampum* was legislated at four beads to the *stiver*, which was the Dutch equivalent of the English penny. However, so many poor quality unstrung beads were put into circulation that in April 1641 a law was passed prohibiting the use of unpolished beads during the month of May. During that month these poorer beads would be accepted in payment of taxes but only if they were strung and then only at the discounted rate of six beads to the stiver. The problems continued, and in May 1650 an ordinance was passed prohibiting the use of loose *wampum*. This law also further discounted poorly made *wampum* that circulated on string, so that they traded at the rate of eight beads to the stiver. As more and more *wampum* flooded the market the value of all beads declined.

In 1661 Director General Stuyvesant addressed the colonists' concern over the steady inflation of *wampum*. Much of it was "unpierced and half-finished, made of stone, bone, glass, shells, horn, nay even of wood, and broken". Huge quantities of this inferior *wampum* was being dumped in the colony by the English with the result that wages and cost of goods rose. Stuyvesant ordered that all wampum used as money must first be strung, and its value was fixed at six white or 3 black beads per *stiver* for high quality trade *wampum*, and eight white or four black beads per *stiver* for inferior quality.

Seawant, or unstrung beads, which had been prohibited from daily commerce in 1650, was still used for tax payments. As late as 1693 commuters on the New York and Brooklyn ferry could pay with either two pence in silver or eight *stivers* in *wampum*. The last recorded exchange of *wampum* as money was in New York in 1701.

HISTORY OF NEW AMSTERDAM

By the mid-1620s, after nearly a decade of trading with the Indians along the river discovered by Henry Hudson, the Dutch decided to establish a permanent presence at the southern end of what is today Manhattan Island. In its first few years, the tiny settlement was little more than a collection of log huts connected by dirt cart paths. There was also a large warehouse in which furs and other trade items were stored; a church, and a handful of other structures. North of the settlement were open fields where sheep and cows grazed, and beyond that were dense woods and rocky outcroppings that extended all the way to the northern tip of the island.

The first ship of settlers to come to New Netherland was the *Eendracht* (Unity), which sailed from Amsterdam on 25 January 1624. On board the ship was an advance party of settlers -- mostly Walloons. Although there is no official passenger list, Joris Rapalje and his bride, Catalyntje Trico were known to be on board. Of the other passengers the only names known are Sebastian Jansen Krol (the comforter of the sick who was sent in lieu of an ordained minister) and John Monfort and his wife Jacqueline Moreau.

In August 1624 the *Eendracht* returned to Amsterdam. Making the return voyage to report on conditions in the infant colony was Krol. He reported that "there are pregnant women there" and asked permission to perform baptisms and marriages upon his return. Two of the pregnant women must have been Adriaentje Cuvelje (since Jan Vigne was the first child to be born in New Netherland) and Catalyntje Trico (since Sarah Rapalje was the "first-born Christian daughter" in the Colony).

A larger contingent of settlers set out for New Netherland on the ship *Nieu Nederlandt* about 1 April 1624 under Cornelius May of Hoorn. It conveyed a colony of thirty families, mostly Walloons. These 30 Walloon families were to establish a colony in America. The *New Netherland* arrived in the bay below Manhattan in early May.

A copy of the original West India Company records gives the full instructions sent over with May on the *New Netherland* for the conduct of the new colony. This paper is dated March 1624, which further fixes the year of the voyage. They were signed by three members of the West India Company. Unfortunately no list of the colonists is given, but on board the second, larger ship was Willem van der Hulst, who later become Director. The well known author and genealogist Zabriskie speculated that others "almost certainly included" Philippe de Trieux, Antone Harduin. Arnould Rhemi and wife Marie Bauldwyn. [27] These names come from dismissals from the Amsterdam Walloon Church for those intending to voyage "to Virginia" which was a catch-all phrase for anyone headed for North America.

Adriaen van der Donck travelled to New Amsterdam in 1641 and several years later published a book called *A Description of the New Netherlands*. This document details the beginnings of New Amsterdam, and was the first book published by a resident of what is now New York State.

The Colony was planted at this time, on the Manhates where a Fort was staked out by Master Kryn Federycke, an engineer. It will be of large dimensions. The ship which has returned home this month brings samples of all the different sorts of produce there. The cargo consists of 7246 Beavers, 675 Otter skins, 48 Minx, 36 Wild cat, and various other sorts; several pieces of oak timber, and hickory.

The counting house there is kept in a stone building, thatched with reed; the other houses are of the bark of trees ... There are thirty ordinary houses on the east side of the river which runs nearly north and south ... Francois Molemaecker is busy building a horse mill, over which shall be constructed a spacious room sufficient to accommodate a large congregation, and then a tower is to be erected where the bells brought from Porto Rico will be hung ...

The document says that, as the fort was being built, ``two hundred and seventy souls, including Men, Women and Children,'' lived in the houses ``in no fear, as the Natives live peaceably with them.'' Van der Donck also attempted to defend the Dutch right to ownership of this land.

That this country was first found or discovered by the Netherlanders is evident and clear from the fact that the Indians or natives of the land, many of whom are still living, and with whom I have conversed, declare freely that before the arrival of the Lowland ship, the Half-Moon, in the year 1609,they did not know that there were any other people in the world than those who were like themselves,much less any people who differed so much in appearance from them as we did ... There are persons who believe that the Spaniards have been here many years ago, when they found the climate too cold to their liking, and again left the country.

He also defined the new Colony's borders: on the north New England, to the south Virginia. West, he wrote, was ``undefined and unknown.''

Many of our Netherlanders have been far into the country, more than seventy or eighty miles from the river and seashore. We also frequently trade with the Indians, who come more than ten or twenty days' journey from the interior, and who have been farther off to catch beavers, and they know of no limits to the country.

The city on Manhattan Island was called New Amsterdam until 1664 when the English took possession. Although passenger lists for the earliest ships to New Amsterdam have been lost, records of later voyages are known.

To the north of the tiny Dutch settlement, the English colony at Plymouth was beginning to grow. Neither liked the presence of the other, and it was only a matter of time before trouble began. Originally the Dutch were looking for trade opportunities and not permanent colonies. They were expanding their economy outward into areas such as sugar, tobacco and the slave trade, which was their real bread and butter. But the growth of the English colonies upset the balance, and endangered their claim to the new lands. They set up their colony at New Amsterdam so they could say they occupied the land and therefore it was theirs.

Partly an offshoot of its slave-trading activities, and partly to meet the labor requirements of the Dutch settlers who carved out large estates in the Hudson River Valley, the Dutch West India Company brought West Africans to New Netherland. 1626 saw the arrival of a ship sailing into New Amsterdam harbour holding 11 African slaves. From the existing Dutch records we can attach names to some of them -- Paul d'Angelo, Simon Congo, Anthony Portugese and John Francisco. Slavery had arrived in New Amsterdam. By 1660 New Netherland's population of roughly 5,000 included around 600 enslaved Africans. [28]

From the time the first settlers arrived in New Amsterdam, religious services had been conducted by laymen in an empty loft above the Grist Mill. With the arrival of Dominie Jonas Michaelius, an ordained minister, in April 1628, the first Protestant church was founded in America. Services continued to be held in the Grist Mill but in 1633 a proper church was built in New Amsterdam. The church, a plain wooden building, faced the East River. Almost ten years later, in 1643, it was replaced by a stone church built within the walls of the Fort. (Fort Amsterdam) The new church had a spire and weathervane that were the first visible objects seen by those sailing inoit the harbour. It was not until 1693 that this church was replaced by another. While the records of this Reformed Dutch Church do not begin until 1639, they provide us with an insight into the lives of these early settlers.

The Dutch had sponsored a good system of primary education under control of the Dutch Reformed Church in schools supported by tuition and taxes. A school had been started in New Amsterdam at least as early as 1638 and by 1644 there was a school in every important town in New Netherland. These semipublic Dutch schools were gradually abandoned after the English conquest, to be replaced by private schools under the auspices of the Anglican Church.[29]

By 1640 the Dutch had hundreds of settlers spread across western Long Island in small, remote farming villages. English settlers were also living in their area. One of the earliest Dutch settlers on Long Island was Joris deRapelje, who in the mid-1620s lived near the present-day Brooklyn Navy Yard. Joris' daughter, Sarah, born in a Dutch village near Albany, was the first white child born in what was to become New York State.

When he arrived in New Amsterdam in May 1647 as the new Director-General to replace William Kieft, Peter Stuyvesant found a colony of approximately 600 diverse individuals in turmoil. Under Kieft, New Netherland had undertaken a ruinous war with the Indians resulting in numerous deaths on both sides. The inhabitants of New Amsterdam disliked Kieft, whose incompetence, they believed, had brought not only the colony but their city of New Amsterdam to the verge of ruin. In protest, the majority of the residents refused to contribute to the upkeep of the town's public works such as the fort and grist mill. The largest and most vital structures for the colony's security and well-being were in advanced states of disrepair.

Stuyvesant shielded Kieft from his attackers while addressing the most serious problems confronting the city. He wrote, "Whereas the fortress New Amsterdam is now and for sometime past . . . greatly decayed, and the walls daily leaped over and more and more trodden underfoot by men and cattle"[30] every male between the ages of 16 and 60 was to work twelve days a year on the maintenance of the fort.[31] By 1654-1655 repairs had advanced to strengthen the walls in response to a threatened attack from the English. However, it was not until 1661 that the fort's walls were entirely faced with stone.[32]

By 1649, Kieft's legacy and Stuyvesant's harsh rule led to increasing dissatisfaction among some of New Amsterdam's leading residents. In the summer of 1649, led by Adriaen van der Donck, who served as secretary to the "Nine Men" Stuyvesant appointed to act as an advisory council, the dissenters prepared a lengthy petition to the Dutch government at The Hague. In addition to describing in detail the promising possibilities of New Netherland, the Remonstrance, as the document was called, sought relief from the administration of the Dutch West India Company and its agent, Peter Stuyvesant.

The petition was received by the States General, the governing body of the Netherlands, in October 1649. This report describes the condition of New Netherland -- the land between the Fresh (Connecticut) and South (Delaware) Rivers, its bountiful resources and potential as a major Dutch colony. The Remonstrance declared that if it were not for the mismanagement of the Dutch West India Company, which van der Donck and his cohorts believed was solely interested in making money for the Company's investors, New Netherland could resist the advancing English who were encroaching from New England to the northand Virginia to the south and prosper. The means to this end was to grant the inhabitants of New Amsterdam their rights as Dutch citizens and to encourage immigration.

To underscore their complaint, the petitioners related the sorry state of New Amsterdam. "The fort under which people will take shelter, and from which it seems, all authority presides, lies like a mole-hill or ruin. It does not contain a single gun carriage, and there is not a piece of canon on a suitable frame, or on a sound platform."[33] Van der Donck also described a windmill in such a state of disrepair that it can only operate with two vanes ". . . the mill is neglected, and having been leaky most of the time, it has become decayed and somewhat rotten, so that it can not now work with anymore than two arms, and has gone on thus for all of five years."[34] The Remonstrance was delivered to the States General on October 13, 1649.

On September 15, 1655, the Peach War erupted with attack on New Amsterdam by a combined force of Manhattan rim Indians. Dozens of farmers, men, women, children, male and female servants sent by Yoncker Henrick van der Capellen to Staten-Island were killed or captured.

For the Dutch this new land was seen as New Netherlands, an extension of the old country. Their villages were Dutch, the language was Dutch, and so were the customs and laws. New Amsterdam looked like a village in the Netherlands. Non-Dutch settlers coming into the area were part of the Dutch system.

In the 17th century a stranger who visited the town of New Amsterdam to wander along the wharves or through the streets, or to loiter beside the canal, or worship in the old church in the fort, or make purchases in the shops of pearl street might have imagined himself in a town of the Netherlands. There were the same houses with stepped gable ends, the same mercantile spirit, the same atmosphere of mingled pettiness and broad tolerance. For a century after the english conquest NewAmsterdam remained largely Dutch.[35]

Special privileges had always been conferred on some inhabitants of cities in the Netherlands, and this was transplanted to New Netherland in the form of Burgher rights. Burgher right gave a citizen freedom of trade, exemption from manual labour, and excemption from being sued by a fellow burgher outside of his burgh. A burgher could not be imprisoned without bail and a limitation of one year was set after which he could not be charged with any offense.

On 2 February 1657 Stuyvesant set forth a decree regarding the Great and Small Burghers. Only Great Burghers could fill public offices and enjoy exemption from confiscation and attainder, if convicted of a capital offense. Stuyvesant's charter declared that all members of the Council, all Burgomasters and Schepens, all Ministers of the Gospel and commissioned officers of militia, past and present, with their descendants in the male line, were automatically Great Burghers. Others might become such also on payment of the sum of 50 guilders into the city treasury.

Small Burghers were entitled only to freedom of trade and to the privilege of being received into their respective Guilds. Natives of the city of New Amsterdam, residents there for a year and six weeks before the date of the charter, burghers' sons-in-law, city store keepers, salaried servants of the Company, and all paying 25 guilders, were entitled to have their names inscribed on the roll of Small Burghers. The Small Burgher Right pertained specifically to the right to keep a shop or to trade in New Amsterdam. The requirements were less stringent and the applicant Small Burgher had to pay a fee of twenty gilders..

Burgher right by descent or inheritance was gained only through the male line. Females might be burghers, but if acquired by purchase, the right was vested in them only while spinsters or widows. They lost it if they remarried those not burghers, but recovered the privilege on decease of such husband. Establishing citizenship was important for they were not otherwise allowed the right to do business in New Amsterdam. [36]

If a person did not 'keep a fire in New Amsterdam for more than four months, he lost his burgher right. This was designed to prevent individuals coming from Albany (a primary example) and setting up shop more or less temporarily. Likewise, the four-month time limit also inhibited the temporary departures of individuals who were significant contributors to the local economy.

In April 1657 it was ordered that those who wanted the Great or Small Burgher right should give their names within eight days or be deprived of their rights. The resulting list is invaluable to researchers, the bulk of names being given between 10 and 18 April, 1657. Additional names were occasionally added through 30 April 1661, presumably reflecting either a newcomer in the town or a young person coming of age and establishing himself in business.

Around this same time frame, the Director-General of the colony informed the Burgomasters that certain defenses were to be made in New Amsterdam in preparation for a possible attack by the English in New England. Guards were to be mounted every night at the tavern and court-house, and the fort had to be repaired. Because the fort could not hold all the citizens of the town, and because there were too many houses to defend, it was also ordered that the main part of the city would be enclosed with palisades and a breastwork from a ditch three feet wide and two feet deep. In case of immediate danger, all families were ordered to gather there. The city needed to raise 6000 guilders to pay for these planned defenses, and the wealthier Burgomasters were expected to lend this money until the community could raise it.

When the English arrived in 1664, the Dutch left, only to return in 1673 for another brief occupancy. New Amsterdam was renamed New York on 8 September 1664 and remained that until 9 August 1673. At that date the name briefly became New Orange. On 10 November1674 it was once more New York - the name this city has been known by ever since.

When the English took possession of the province in 1664 the total population did not exceed 8,000, and of these a large proportion were not Dutch at all but French Flemings, Walloons and English. Yet New Netherlands was predominantly Dutch, not only in its political institutions, but in blood, language, customs, industry, agricultures, education, agriculture, religion.[37]

BOELE AND BAYKEN IN NEW NETHERLAND

Baptismal records confirm that the three children on the passenger list of the Otter which brought the family to the New World in 1659 were Aefje baptised 1655 (age 3), Jacob baptised 1657 (age 2) and Abraham baptised 1658 (the nursing child). The 14 year old boy accompanying them has not been identified.

Two more children were born to Boele and Bayken after they settled in New Amsterdam: Hendrick baptised 6 February 1661 [38] and Tryntie baptised 8 October 1662. [39]

The family group consists of:

Boele Roelofszen born circa 1625, from Uffelte (modern spelling) in Drenthe, Netherlands, married 10 May 1654 in Amsterdam to Bayken Arents, baptised 21 March 1621 in Amsterdam, the daughter of Arents Pietersz and Aechjen Heinrixdr.; they emigrated to New Netherland in 1659.

In 1660 a map showing property owners and their occupations notes Lot 26 was owned by Boele Roeloffsen, tailor. [40]

Children:

1. Aefje, baptised 22 March 1655 Amsterdam m. 31 March 1675 New York, Dirck Ten Eyck, [41]son of Abraham Ten Eyck and Maria Boele.[42]
2. Jacob, bap. 25 April 1657 Amsterdam, m. 21 May 1679 New York, Catharina Clock, [43]daughter of Abraham Martense Clock and Tryntje Alberts. [44]
3. Abram, bap. 11 Dec. 1658 Amsterdam (probably died in New Netherland as a child).
4. Hendrick, bap. 6 Feb. 1661 New Amsterdam, m. 3 Feb. 1686 New York, Anneken Coert, [45]daughter of Barent Courten and Annetje Jans. [46]
5. Tryntie, bap. 8 Oct. 1662 New Amsterdam, bethrothed 2 April 1682 New York, to Willem Hellikers, [47]son of Jacob Hellikers alias Swart and Teuntje Theunis. [48]

In May 1681 Boele and several other men were given the right to sell a house in New York on behalf of Trijntje Harmes, wife of Jacob Jansz Doens. Jacob was a slave in Nigeria, and Trijntje was the only heir of her cousin Anna Kocks who had recently died in New ork. The fact that Trijntje gave power of attorney to the men indicates they were trustworthy individuals. The full text of the document follows.

Inventory Notary P. de Wit [49] May 10th 1681

Trijntje Harmens, the housewife of Jacob Jansz Doens, declares to the notary that she is the only heiress of her cousin Anna Kocks, who died in New York. Trijntje has become her heiress because Anna's son Gallas Kocks died in Amsterdam.

Trijntje gives procuration to Captain Marten Kriger, Pieter Stoutenburg, Mr. [50] Nicolaas Beijert , Hendrick Willem van Jeveren [51] and Boel Roeloffsz (all of them living in New York) to claim and sell a house and premises in New York that Trijntje inherited from her cousin. Because Trijntje's husband Jacob Jansz Doens is held in captivity as a slave in Algeria, her guardian is now Cornelis Ruijven instead of her husband.

Present as witnesses are: Claas Verbraack, skipper on the ship called '*de Goutsblom*' (the Goldflower) and Jacob Maurits skipper on the ship called '*de Bever*' (the Beaver).

The fact that Trijntje Harmens gave power of attorney to the above mentioned men tells us that the appointed men were trustworthy people.

Estate of GALLAS KOCK [52], deceased, February 17, 1680/1.

To Nicholas Bayard to ballance his accompt 291. 5 Florins
To the Deacons of the Dutch Church 450. Florins
To Hans Kiersted to ballance 190. Florins
To the Treasurer of this city 28. Florins
Total 959. 5 Florins

In persuance of an order from the Worshipfull Mayors Court of January 30, directed to us to examine and make up the accounts of Mr. Martin Cregier and Mr. Peter Stoutenburgh, the Trustees of estate of Gallas Kock. In obedience whereof we have examined the same, and find the estate as more at large set
forth.

Your Humble Servants,
NICHOLAS BAYARD, P. DELANOY.

Credited by Francis Lovelance, for ballance for House rent 814. 3 Florins.
Peter Grovendyke, ballance of House rent 427. 7 Florins.
Elders of Dutch Church, ballance of House rent till the first of May next

By one dwelling house and lot of ground, situate and lying within this city of New York, on the Broadway, next to the house and lot of Martin Cregier, as more at large may appear by the Patent and other Papers. (No value given.)

TRYNTIE ARENTS & GERRIT JANSEN ROOS

Tryntie Arents was baptised 18 January 1629 in Amsterdam to father Arent Pietersz. She was Bayken Arents' sister and came to New Netherland with Bayken's family in 1659 on the ship Otter.

Shortly after her arrival she married the widower Gerrit Jansen Roos. Their intentions were recorded in the Reformed Dutch Church of New Amsterdam as:

1659. 5 Sept. Gerrit Janszen, Wedr. Van Aeltje Lamberts, en Tryntje Arents, Van Amsterdam.

Children with Tryntje Arents:

1663. 8 Apr; Gerrit Janszen Roos, Tryntie Arents; **David**; Boele Roelofszen, Marritie Geleyns
1665. 10 Apr; Gerrit Janszen Roos, Tryntie Arents; **Aefje**; Boelen Roelofszen, Emerensje Van Zluys, Bayken Arents
1667. 27 Feb; Gerrit Janszen Roos, Tryntie Arents; **Aeltie**; Jan Vinge, Tryntie Roelofs

Gerrit's marriage to Aeltje Lamberts took place in New Amsterdam in 1651

1651 31 Dec; **Gerrit Janszen**, jm van Haerlem; **Aeltje Lamberts**, jd van Uytrecht

Children with Aeltje Lamberts:

1653. **Pieter** 19 Jan; Gerrit Janszen, Aeltje Lamberts; Pieter; Abraham Planck, Jan Vinge, Maria Planck
1655. **Cornelia** 1 Jan; Gerrit Janszen; Cornelia; Emmetie Van der Sluys
1656. **Johannes** 5 Nov; Gerrit Janszen Roos, Aeltje Lamberts; Johannes; Abigail Planck

On August 16, 1654 Gerrit, a carpenter, and Pieter Pietersen van Nest sued Jan Coopal for the balance due on a house they built for him.

Per New Amsterdam Orphan Court records: "Garrit Janzen Roos announces death of his wife, who left him with three children, Pieter, 6 years old, Cornelia, 4 years old, Johannes, 2 years old. He accepts as guardian, Abraham Verplanck and Jan Vigne. Wednesday, June 8, 1659."

Gerrit's will was dated 3 Sep 1697; he died by 15 Sep 1698.

In the name of God, Amen, this 3rd day of September, 1697. I, Gerritt Jansen Roos of the city of New York, carpenter, being in sound mind and perfect health, I leave to my eldest son Peter Roos, living at Utrecht in Holland, £100. I leave to Peter Gerritse Roos, the eldest son of my son Peter Roos, one silver tumbler and the same to Gerritt Johannes Roos, the eldest son of Johannes Roos. Also a silver tumbler to Gerritt Provost, the eldest son of my eldest daughter Cornelia, wife of Elias Provost. I leave to Gerritt Johannes Roos and Aeltje Roos, children of my deceased son Johannes Roos, their maintenance out of my estate until they are able to maintain themselves and they are to be put to school until such time as they shall have learned to read and write, and they are to have £78 which I have of their father's estate. The rest of the estate to be divided into five parts and given to son Peter, the children of son Johannes, deceased, to daughter Cornelia, wife of Jacob De Moree, to daughter Affie, wife of Johannes Van Gelder, and to Annatie Elswort, daughter of my daughter Aeltie procured by John Elswort. And whereas I have sold a house and lot in Albany, which belonged to my son Johannes, and also a tract of land in said county for £78, the children of my son Johannes are to have the same. Executors: Jacob De Moree, Johannes Van Gelder and Jacob Boden.

GEN 2 AEFJE BOELEN & DIRCK TEN EYCK

Aefje, baptised 22 March 1655 Amsterdam married 31 March 1675 New York, Dirck Ten Eyck, [53]son of Abraham Ten Eyck and Maria Boele.[54]

Dirck was baptised in Amsterdam in the Oude Kerk (Old Church) on 27 October 1658

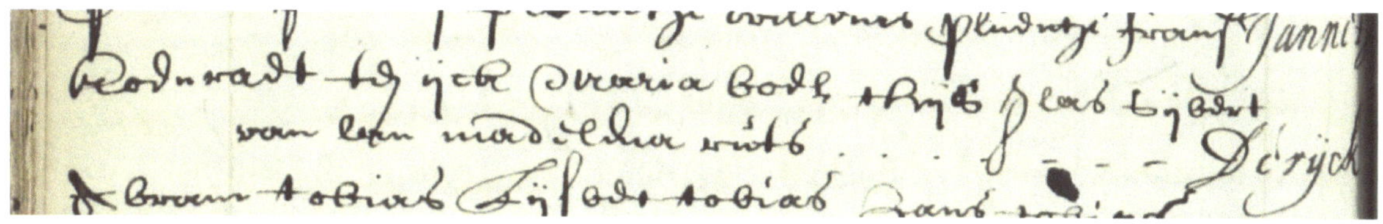

Derijck - 27-10-1648 - Oude Kerk - Hervormd - [ten] IJck, Koenraet - Boel, Maria - [55]

Children:

1676. Andries. 22 Jul; Dirck ten Eyck, Aefje Boelen; Andries; Coenraedt ten Eyck, Bayken Boelen [Aefje's mother] [56]
1678. Jacob. 14 Nov; Dirck ten Eyck, Aefje Boelen; Jacob; Boele Roelofszen [Aefje's father],Belitje Hercx [57]
1681. Andries. 4 May; Dirck ten Eyck, Aefje Boelen; Andries; Tobias ten Eyck, Tryntie Boelen [Aefje's sister] [58]
1684. Coenradt. 15 Jun; Dirck ten Eyck, Aefje Boelen; Coenraet; Coenraet ten Eyck, Catharina Clock [59]
1686. Maryken. 19 Dec; Dirck ten Eyck, Aefje Boelen; Maryken; Jacob Boelen, Bayken ______ [probably Bayken Arents, mother of Aefje] [60]
1689. Maryken. 10 Feb; Dirck ten Eyck, Aefje Boelen; Maryken; Hendrick Boelen, Annetje Court [61]
1691. Abraham. 15 Jun; Dirck ten Eyck, Aefje Boelen; Abraham; Willem Helleken [Aefje's brother-in-law], Lysbeth Hegeman [62]
1694. Dirck. 25 Dec; Dirck ten Eyck, Aefje Boelens; Dirck; Boele Roelofszen, Petronella ten Eyck [63]

GEN 2 JACOB BOELEN & CATHARINA CLOCK

Jacob, baptised 25 April 1657 Amsterdam, married 21 May 1679 New York, Catharina Clock, [64]daughter of Abraham Martense Clock and Tryntje Alberts. [65]

Children:

1680. Bayken 14 Jul; Jacob Boelen, Catharina Klock; Bayken; Boele Roelofszen [Jacob's father], Tryntie Klock [66]
1685. Isaac. 20 Dec; Jacob Boelen, Catharina Klock; Isaac; Boele Roelofszen [Jacob's father], Aefje Boelen [Jacob's sister] [67]
1688. Tryntje. 16 Apr; Jacob Boelen, Catharina Klock; Tryntie; Albert Klock, Tryntie Boelen [Jacob's sister] [68]
1690. Jacob 6 Apr; Jacob Boelen, Catharina Klock; Jacob; Dirck ten Eyck, Lysbeth Van der Heul [69]
1692. Catharina. 28 Aug; Jacob Boelen, Catharina Klock; Catharina; Daniel Rappailje, Annetje Barents [70] She married Jacob Goulet
1697. Henrikus. 5 May; Jacob Boele, Catharina Klok; Henrikus; Willem Hellaken, Tryntje Van der Heul wife of Albert Klok [71]

Surviving records in Marbletown, New York, indicate that the silversmith Jacob Boelen was hired in 1704 to make the town seal shown above.

GEN 2 HENDRICK BOELEN & ANNEKEN COERT

Hendrick, baptised 6 February 1661 New Amsterdam, married 3 Feb. 1686 New York, Anneken Coert, [72]daughter of Barent Courten and Annetje Jans. [73]

Children:

1686. Anna. 28 Nov; Hendrick Boelenszen, Anneken Kourt; Anna; Boelen Roelofszen [Hendrick's father], Christina Wessels [74]
1688. Abraham. 1 Aug; Hendrick Boelen, Anneken Court; Abraham; Barent Court, Aefje Boelen [75]

Hendrick was a gunsmith. When he died in 1691 at age 30, he left a wife and son to be cared for by his extended family. In his will he named four tutors and overseers to see to Abraham's education – his father Boele Roeloffsen, his brother Jacob Boelen, and his two brothers-in-law Willem Hellikers and Dirck Ten Eyck.

Page 390.—HENDRICK (or HENRY) BOELEN. "Know all men by these presents, that I, Henry Boelen, of New York, smith, being sick and weak. I leave to my wife, Antie Berents, the use of all my estate during her life, and she shall give to her son Alexander, when of age, such portion as she can conveniently spare, and after her decease he is to be sole heir, and if he should die the estate to go to Boelen Roeloffs, my father. If my wife should remarry she shall secure to my son Abraham Boelen £125, and he is to be instructed to read and write, and afterwards to learn a trade by which he shall live in the future. He is also to have my great Dutch Bible as a particular gift and legacy." Makes Roeler Roeloffen, Jacob Boelen, Dirck Ten Eyck tutors and overseers, and his wife executor.

Dated May 15, 1691. Witnesses, A. De Lanoy, P. De Lanoy.

New York, December 10, 1691, there appeared before me, being authorized by Governor-General Benjamin Fletcher, the above named witnesses, and made oath to the same, that they saw Henry Boelen sign and seal the same. David Jamieson, Dep. Sec.

[NOTE.—Antie Boelen, the widow, married Abraham Kettletas, December 10, 1692.]

76

GEN 2 TRYNTIE BOELEN & WILLIAM HELLIKERS (HELLAKENS)

Tryntie, baptised 8 Oct. 1662 New Amsterdam, bethrothed 2 April 1682 New York, to Willem Hellikers, [77]son of Jacob Hellikers alias Swart and Teuntje Theunis. [78]

Willem was dead by 1 October 1702 when his will was read. Note that "Tryntje" is the diminuitie of "Catherine/Katherine".

Whereas, WILLIAM HELLIKER, lately deceased, leaving behind him a will, declaring his wife Katharine sole executrix, which said Katharine has lately died, since the decease of her husband, and without proving the said will, Therefore Jacob Boelen, silversmith, and Dirck Ten Eyck, cordwainer, uncles and guardians of Katharine, Maritse, and Aphia, children of said William Helliker, by Katharine, his wife, deceased, are made administrators, during the minority of the children, October 1, 1702.

Page 320.—Inventory of estate of WM. HELLIKER, taken at the request of Alderman Jacob Baelen and Dirck Ten Eyck, October 5, 1702. House and lot, £250. ¼ of a house on Broad st., £50. 3 pieces of 8, 18s. Johanes Van Gelder, Wm. Huddlestone.

This account was exhibited as a just and true account of the administration of the estate of Wm. Helliker, deceased, by Jacob Boelen and Dirck Ten Eyck, administrators, March 23, 170⅔. Cornbury.

[79]

Children:

1683. Jacob. 7 Mar; Willem Jacobszen, Tryntie Boelen; Jacob; Boele Roelofszen [Tryntje's father], Teuntie Idens [80]
1685. Bayken 24 Jan; Willem Hellaecken, Tryntie Boelen; Bayken; Jacob Boelen [Tryntje's brother], Bayken Arents [Tryntje's mother] [81]
1687. Dina. 13 Mar; Willem Hellakens, Tryntie Boelen; Dina; Dirck ten Eyck, Geesje Idens [82]
1689. Tryntje 31 Mar; Willem Hellaken, Tryntie Boelen; Tryntie; Hendrick Boelen, Aefje Boelen [83]
1691. Bayken. 25 Oct; Willem Helleken, Tryntje Boelens; Bayken; Boelen Roelofszen [Tryntje's father], Catharina Klock [84]
1694. Hendrick. 11 Mar; Willem Hellaken, Tryntie Boelen; Hendrick; Boelen Roelofszen [Tryntje's father], Aefje ten Eyck [Tryntje's sister] [85]

1697. Willem. 4 Apr; Willem Hellaken, Tryntje Boelen; Willem; Boele Roelofs [Tryntje's father], Teuntje Theunis Wed: van Jan Stryker [86]
1699. Maria. 15 Oct; Willem Helhake, Tryntje Boele; Maria; Jacob Boelen [Tryntje's brother], Rebecca Idese wife of Adrian Van Schaick [87]
1702. Aefje 18 Mar; Willem Helhakers, Tryntie Boele; Aefje; Jacob Boele, Aefje Boele wife of Dirk Ten Yk [88]

ENDNOTES

[1] REC. 72:265-94
[2] N.Y. Colonial MSS. Book KK p. 21 indicates that Boele sailed on the Otter, arriving on 17 Feb. 1659. The published lists in "Ship Passenger Lists, New York and New Jersey (1600-1825)" edited and indexed by Carl Boyer, 3rd. (Westminster, MD: Family Line Publications, 1978) pages 119-120 incorrectly assigns Boele to the previous ship, De Trouw.
[3] "Records of the Reformed Dutch Church in New Amsterdam and New York; Marriages from 11 December 1639 to 29 August 1801", compiled by Samuel S. Purple, M.D. (New York Genealogical and Biographical Society, Collections, Volume 1, 1890) (Hereafter called RDCMarrPurple) p. 24 REC. 72:266. "Betrothed 5 Sept. 1659. Gerrit Janszen, Wedr. Van Aeltje Lamberts, en Tryntje Arents, Van Amsterdam"
[4] New World Immigrants: A Consolidation of Ship Passenger Lists and Associated Data from Periodical Literature edited by Michael Tepper. Volume 1:172
[5] RDCMarrPurple: pp 40, 45

[7] There is no other Uffelte in the Netherlands, and records from there are not available. The closest town of Hoogeveen does not have baptismal church records before 1685.
[8] hereafter referred to as GAA
[9] Amssterdam DTB (473/159), Marriage Notices in the Nieuwe Kerk
[10] A journeyman tailor is someone who is still being supervised by a master tailor.
[11] DTB 473, p.159 - Huwelijksintekeningen van de KERK. - OTR00050000083
[12] Amsterdam DTB (990/288), Marriages in the Nieuwe Kerk
[13] Amsterdam DTB (43/299), Baptisms in the Nieuwe Kerk
[14] DTB 43, p.299 - 000000041971
[15] Amsterdam DTB (43/354), Baptisms in the Nieuwe Kerk
[16] DTB 43, p.354 - 000000041999
[17] Amsterdam DTB (43/399), Baptisms in the Nieuwe Kerk
[18] DTB 43, p.399 – 000000042020
[19] Amsterdam DTB (139/86), Baptisms in the Lutheran Church
[20] Amsterdam DTB (5/348), Baptisms in the Oude Kerk
[21] DTB 5, p.348 - Ber: va. Kaffawerker. - A28217000180
[22] According to Pim Nieuwenhuis "kaffa" is an Indian [meaning from the Dutch East Indies] multi-coloured cotton
[23] Amsterdam DTB (139/268), Baptisms in the Lutheran Kerk
[24] DTB 139, p.268 - 000000062097
[25] DTB 414, p.314 - Huwelijksintekeningen van de KERK. - OTR00009000167
[26] SLC film 0113186. 414/314
[27] George Olin Zabriskie wrote about the Rapalje family in his series, "The Founding Families of New Netherland" in The Halve Maen: January, April, July 1972
[28] Wood, Betty. The Origins of American Slavery: Freedom and Bondage in the English Colonies A Critical Issue. New York: Hill and Wang, c1997 pp 132
[29] The Colonial America, Second Edition by Oscar Theodore Barck, Jr. and Hugh Talmage Leflter, 1968, p. 409-412
[30] Stokes, Vol. IV, p. 110
[31] Stokes, Vol. IV, p. 112
[32] Stokes, Vol. IV, p. 214
[33] Adriaen vander Donck et al, Remonstrance of New Netherland, O'Callaghan, Vol. I, p. 303
[34] O'Callaghan, Vol. I, p. 299

[35] The Founding of American Civilization: The Middle Colonies by Thomas Jefferson Wertenbaker, 1963. pp 35-36
[36] The New York Historical Society: Collections 1885 (subtitled, Burghers and Freemen), pages 1-35. Courtesy of Ruth Piwanka
[37] The Founding of American Civilization: The Middle Colonies by Thomas Jefferson Wertenbaker, 1963. pp 35-36
[38] Baptisms from 1639 to 1730 in the Reformed Dutch Church, New York City, Vol. 2 NYG&BS Colls., 1901, pp 59,66
[39] ibid
[40] Vol. II pp 215-341 of I.N. Phelps Stokes: The Iconography of Manhattan Island 1498-1909, Arno Press, NY, 1967, 6 Volumes by Robert L. Protzmann, April 1999. Lot Numbers are based on "The Key to the Castello Plan" as provided by Stokes. The Dutch grants map uses a different lot numbering system. Likewise the Castello Plan, by Spiers, also uses a different system of numbering.
[41] RDCMarrPurple: p. 40
[42] For Aefjie's descendants see Rec. 63:152-155, 118:14-16; Maria Boele probably was not related to Boele Roeloffszen, see Rec. 72: 294, 118:16-18 for her family.
[43] RDCMarrPurple: p. 45
[44] For Jacob's descendants see Rec. 72:267f. Catharina was bap. 18 Jan. 1654 New Amsterdam (Baptisms from 1639 to 1730, p. 36; mother's patronymic given at baptism of her sister, ibid., p. 43). For an account of the Clocks see William A. Eardeley, Chronology and Ancestry of Chauncey M. Depew (1918), pp 211-12.
[45] RDCMarrPurple: p. 59
[46] For Hendrick's descendants see Rec. 72:268f. Anneken was bap. 20 Oct. 1666 new Amsterdam (Baptisms from 1639 to 1730 p 85); for her family see Rec. 44:326.
[47] RDCMarrPurple: p. 50
[48] For Tryntie's descendants see Rec. 72:269f. For Willem Hellikers see also Rec. 121:18.
[49] Notarial Archives inv. 4959 folio 453-454, GAA (Gemeentearchief Amsterdam)
[50] Mr. is a Dutch abbreviation for someone who has a degree in Law
[51] Van Every
[52] Abstracts of Wills Vol II 1708-1728, pages 423 & 424:
[53] RDCMarrPurple: p. 40
[54] For Aefjie's descendants see Rec. 63:152-155, 118:14-16; Maria Boele probably was not related to Boele Roeloffszen, see Rec. 72: 294, 118:16-18 for her family.
[55] DTB 8, p.184 - 000000034383
[56] https://www.olivetreegenealogy.com/nn/church/rdcbapt_1676.shtml
[57] https://www.olivetreegenealogy.com/nn/church/rdcbapt_1678.shtml
[58] https://www.olivetreegenealogy.com/nn/church/rdcbapt_1681.shtml
[59] https://www.olivetreegenealogy.com/nn/church/rdcbapt_1684.shtml
[60] https://www.olivetreegenealogy.com/nn/church/rdc_bp168690.shtml
[61] https://www.olivetreegenealogy.com/nn/church/rdc_bp168690.shtml
[62] https://www.olivetreegenealogy.com/nn/church/rdc_bp169195.shtml
[63] https://www.olivetreegenealogy.com/nn/church/rdc_bp169195.shtml
[64] RDCMarrPurple: p. 45
[65] For Jacob's descendants see Rec. 72:267f. Catharina was bap. 18 Jan. 1654 New Amsterdam (Baptisms from 1639 to 1730, p. 36; mother's patronymic given at baptism of her sister, ibid., p. 43). For an account of the Clocks see William A. Eardeley, Chronology and Ancestry of Chauncey M. Depew (1918), pp 211-12.
[66] https://www.olivetreegenealogy.com/nn/church/rdcbapt_1680.shtml

[67] https://www.olivetreegenealogy.com/nn/church/rdcbapt_1685.shtml
[68] https://www.olivetreegenealogy.com/nn/church/rdc_bp168690.shtml
[69] https://www.olivetreegenealogy.com/nn/church/rdc_bp168690.shtml
[70] https://www.olivetreegenealogy.com/nn/church/rdc_bp169195.shtml
[71] https://www.olivetreegenealogy.com/nn/church/rdcbapt_1697.shtml
[72] RDCMarrPurple: p. 59
[73] For Hendrick's descendants see Rec. 72:268f. Anneken was bap. 20 Oct. 1666 new Amsterdam (Baptisms from 1639 to 1730 p 85); for her family see Rec. 44:326.
[74] https://www.olivetreegenealogy.com/nn/church/rdc_bp168690.shtml
[75] https://www.olivetreegenealogy.com/nn/church/rdc_bp168690.shtml
[76] Abstracts of Wills on File in the Surrogate's Office: City of New York. 1892
[77] RDCMarrPurple: p. 50
[78] For Tryntie's descendants see Rec. 72:269f. For Willem Hellikers see also Rec. 121:18.
[79] Abstracts of Wills on File in the Surrogate's Office: City of New York. 1892
[80] https://www.olivetreegenealogy.com/nn/church/rdcbapt_1683.shtml
[81] https://www.olivetreegenealogy.com/nn/church/rdcbapt_1685.shtml
[82] https://www.olivetreegenealogy.com/nn/church/rdc_bp168690.shtml
[83] https://www.olivetreegenealogy.com/nn/church/rdc_bp168690.shtml
[84] https://www.olivetreegenealogy.com/nn/church/rdc_bp169195.shtml
[85] https://www.olivetreegenealogy.com/nn/church/rdc_bp169195.shtml
[86] https://www.olivetreegenealogy.com/nn/church/rdcbapt_1697.shtml
[87] https://www.olivetreegenealogy.com/nn/church/rdcbapt_1699.shtml
[88] https://www.olivetreegenealogy.com/nn/church/rdcbapt_1702.shtml

www.ingramcontent.com/pod-product-compliance
Lightning Source LLC
LaVergne TN
LVHW070151110826
845147LV00002B/374

* 9 7 8 1 9 8 7 9 3 8 2 9 6 *